Veiled Nightmares

&

Ethereal Dreams

Ian McGrath

Beaten Track

www.beatentrackpublishing.com

Veiled Nightmares and Ethereal Dreams

First published 2022 by Beaten Track Publishing
Copyright © 2022 Ian McGrath

Paperback ISBN: 978 1 78645 518 5
eBook ISBN: 978 1 78645 519 2

Beaten Track Publishing,
Burscough, Lancashire.
www.beatentrackpublishing.com

Foreword by Ali Harwood

A few years ago, I asked Ian McGrath to be one of our first featured poets at the Liver Bards monthly poetry event I host in Liverpool. The evening was titled 'Sun' and Ian surely shone. My review of his set rings true today, including the line 'he took us to the precipice as a traveller and a troubadour but then showed us the light'. As a poet, he has journeyed far and wide since then and has documented these often challenging times and sometimes uplifting moments in verse.

Ian's words in *Veiled Nightmares & Ethereal Dreams* take us through troubled waters but there are pools of hope here, too. In the titles of the nine chapters of this collection, including 'Angels and Demons', 'Life', 'Death' and 'Rebirth', the reader can already appreciate the elemental concerns of their creator: this poet lives and breathes and feels the extremes of human emotions.

In 'Life Support', the narrator seems to yearn for a togetherness within an intimate relationship which may not last as they plummet to the ground. However, as 'the land dies', there is a glint of something better as we read that 'life will find a way'.

Have you ever fought your mind? Direct questions such as this confront you in the poem 'Depression'. Then, we read the reality of the misery involved when in this state.

Although painful to read, the sharing of these vulnerable truths make Ian's work resonate.

This collection is bookended with poems of nightmares and dreams. Between the covers, Ian reveals that he is awake to the storms that taunt us and haunt us. He also gives us more than a glimpse that his eyes are willing to search for something brighter.

Veiled Nightmares & Ethereal Dreams is at once intense, lyrical and honest. I recommend you dive into these pages to explore its turbulent depths and experience its glimmers of light. Threading throughout its course, Ian's powerful poetic voice radiates.

Ali Harwood is an artist, poet, writer and teacher based in Liverpool, UK. He enjoys working locally, nationally and internationally. Ali's visual art has been exhibited and commissioned throughout Merseyside and beyond for many years. His poetry is widely performed and published and he appreciates collaborating with dancers, musicians and fellow poets. Ali writes for both children and adults and his work as a teacher is broad and varied, ranging from tutoring individuals to collaborating with educational organisations and local authorities.

Prologue

I have been writing poetry for over a decade now; I spend a lot of time writing it, though not as much as I'd like these days. When I think about those first poems I wrote and the work I had to put into each one to get them to say what I wanted in the right way, it puts the whole journey into perspective. I had advice from two close friends to me, two brothers who had completely opposing opinions on how to approach the task of writing a poem. One brother (the older) thought that you should agonise over every syllable and go back through it countless times until it has that flowing water kind of feel. The younger brother felt that you should not go over the poetry and edit it, as the process is a way of working through your troubles; he believed that each place where it stuck or didn't flow right was a point where you were working through something, and the lack of flow in a poem shows the lack of harmony or unity in the emotions or problems you were working through and processing. I think that the poems where you don't finish or quite get them down as an accurate translation of what you wanted to say are what leads the problems to clear so that the next poem you write flows and is finished easily, accurately reflecting your thoughts and needing very little in the way of editing.

I like the metaphor of seeing it as a flowing river, and the places where it sticks are like the rocks the river must flow through or over. I often turn to poetry when I am troubled or have problems, also when I am happy, drunk, manic, depressed, tired. Sometimes I write none for a while and then write several all at once; but what does it all mean to me, and where has it got me? As I write this now, I think it has probably been one of the greatest things I have discovered on my journey, a way of externalising internal problems and turning negatives into positives. The translation along my arm through either pen or keyboard, while not exact, helps to translate my thoughts into a more usable form. I often these days, need to make only very small changes to the poems that I write, although at times when I am struggling the most, my flow can sometimes be off by the most. Then again, sometimes I do my best work and flow most easily when I have a big life problem to deal with.

I like to see poetry as an imprint of a moment, but whereas a photograph or picture captures the look of a place that you visited or the age and smile of the person in that picture. I see poetry as an imprint or fingerprint of a moment in the mind: it is a way of storing emotion and feelings so that you can come back to it later and remember how you felt or where you were that day and where your life was. Each of these poems is important to me and each of these categories is a subject I have explored throughout my journey as a poet. I hope through sharing them that those who read them will gain something from the sharing of my experience and my journey. I have written perhaps a thousand or more finished and edited pieces throughout my time; some work, some don't. Some I like one day and ignore the next, but I like to go back to them anyway and to think about the state of mind I was in when it was written and what it means for me in the present moment or what it tells me of my path going forwards.

Before we move on to the poetry, I wanted to just put some words down about the cover itself. By some happy accident, the picture of my dreamcatcher has ended up being the cover of this book. It wasn't the first or only choice, but I think it's great that it has ended up the cover. I've suffered terrible nightmares and strong dreams throughout my entire life. As I grew into my teens, I used to sleep with my eyes open and I still talk in my sleep when stressed. My grandfather bought me a dreamcatcher to help with those nightmares and it seemed to work. I was bullied and depressed in high school, and I made myself a promise to become a writer when I left school.

Fast forward to my adult life, and I now mostly have a handle on my sleep, dreams and general happiness. I was in the loft of my house searching for camping gear to go to Glastonbury Festival with my friends when I spied the dreamcatcher. I hung it up near the blinds of the bay window of my room which overlooked the large trees at the end of the driveway. That night, I went to sleep and I had a dream that I became a successful author and writer. It raises that question even in a sceptic like myself – that there really could be a spiritual side out there which we cannot understand and explain. Dreams really can be a mysterious focal point for such things.

Categories

Life

The Nightmare in my Dreams

Asleep, awake, alive I dream,
Where nothing's as it seems,
I cannot get away from this,
I'm alive in pain and bliss.
I see an angel come to me,
On her wings so bright and free
From the far-lands of my mind,
Hither on those winds to find.
She fills the time of day and night,
My morning and my evening,
A welcome, haunting, sweet delight,
She's with me now I'm grieving.
In the day between each visit,
I am lost to thoughts of her,
I wander depths of thought and spirit,
I see her everywhere.

She comes to me in strands of light,
In the folds that lie between,
She cuts reality at the seam,
She wields the very night.
The nightmare forms real as she,
The dark takes hold my soul,
Deaf to every desperate plea,
To return the dreams she stole.
I'm calling as I'm tumbling,
Falling deep into my slumber,
I wish to see her face again,
In my waking eyes and brain.
And in the silence of her hateful stare,
I'll feel that shining glare.

Autumn Dance

Come with me away,
On a wet and windy day,
To the burning red forest,
Where fairies often rest,
Here the leaves all die,
They fall and catch the eye,
Dancing in the wind,
Storm clouds flash and sing,
Raindrops patter around,
Music from the ground,
The dance of autumn death,
Saves life for spring breath,
Come to there with me,
We'll dance so wild and free,

Here the mushrooms grow,

Pick the ones we know,

We'll paint across the sky,

Let's never ever die,

So come with me to dance,

This might be your last chance,

In falling burning leaves,

As the land dies and breathes,

In red and orange fire,

Burns truth of death's desire,

Know that life will find a way,

When winter's had its day.

Life Support

Do I fall enough, with all my love,
From heights to way beneath me?
It opens up, so high above,
The ground gives way too easily.

My lungs give way to me, my love,
My heart pumps on in vain,
As I fall, I've had enough,
The cycle begins again.

Support me now, please help me through,
The long night so weak and feeble,
Fold me in your wings so true,
Fly as angel or an eagle.

So far below, beneath our love,
The wonder of the Earth,
There to break our fall, it's tough,
The place where we were birthed.

My mind has stopped, my heart no more,
My soul is damaged too,
There's nothing now of which I'm sure,
Except that I loved you.

So fall with me or fall alone,
Through every empty yard,
For all the things we can't atone,
Our crash will be so hard.

So pull the plug and let me go,
My life support has ended,
With all I leave, please just know,
I'm glad we were befriended.

With all my love, and all that love,
With all the heart can muster,
Please go my love, you'll soar above,
Shining in your lustre.

I tried and failed, to no avail,
My mind and matter break,
I no longer hope we will prevail,
As I reach all I could take.

Cherish

The budding green of life grows blooming and serene,
A melody and symphony sets a wondrous scene.

You feel another chance at life to grow and to evolve,
The pain and fear that held you, oh, so quickly they dissolve.

The shoots are taking off, and they are gripping pain and fear,
Feel the healing guide you as you smile from ear to ear.

The highs and lows of summer and the feel of passing breeze,
The change is very subtle as it flows through moving trees.

The night has come to claim me, the darkness knows my name,
The moon is here to guide me, silvered light is here to tame.

I sit amongst the starlight knowing right where I reside,
Like suspended crystal vials, in their light I cannot hide.

Glittering around me, fairy dust across the sky,
I see my reflection looking back when lost in another's eyes.

I see the look of life and feel the magic of their soul,
I accept I am a part, that I am half and not a whole.

So with the touch of skin to hand, I feel a need to feel your veins,
The life that flows in me, it flows in you all just the same.

So feel the warmth of breath, of condensation and of sweat,
The friction of your skin to theirs this night has no regrets.

The moment came to guide us, in its grasp we can be free,
Enveloped in the darkness we find hope and we break free.

So when the trees are stripped and bare, out in the naked night,
The birds have all flown fast away, with cold behind their flight.

When winter's breath is on us and we try but cannot stand,
Find again this moment and find still across the land.

Fall in love with a moment, with the morning when you wake,
Be proud of all the torments you have faced as breath you take.

Draw the life-force in as it fills all your lungs and core,
Be sure that something guides you and you can be so much more.

Grasp it as you conquer pain, the times you felt dismayed,
Cherish every hope and dream the journey that you made.

The Changing Face of Love

These are the changing times of life,
The moving sands of fate,
This is the walk of heavy strife,
The shifting grudge and hate.

They are the grasping hands of comfort,
The face that comes again,
In my mind, my dreams contort,
There's a goddess in my brain.

She soothes my inner thoughts,
She knows my every weakness,
By her will, I am caught,
She lifts the shrouding bleakness.

She bears the changing heart of woe,
Healing hands and holy chalice,
To dream is all I know,
Tear me away from malice.

She wears the changing face of love,
And the silk of worlds gone by,
On angel wings from above,
She soothes my mind's eye.

The greed and sins are gone,
My past shall be forgiven,
I'll return to be as one,
With the help that she has given.

Tree of Life

The tree of life towers,
Leaves and blooming flowers,
Come see its shining fruit,
Mountains beneath its roots,
Rivers feed to its bough,
Punctured sky just asks how,
Glowing angels on top,
Growing branches won't stop,
It gives the gift of life,
Cuts the land like a knife,
From this all life does stem,
The gift it gives to men,
Eternal green garden,
Link of life and Eden,
Fruit to bear all our sins,
Space to spread all their wings,
Here divinity lives,
Where Trinity's grace gives,
All flows eternally,
Souls heal internally,
Spreads life through glory's seed,
Let all know we are freed,
Relying on its breath,
Undying beyond death.

Praying for Clouds

I was praying for clouds, for the gods to smite with lightning,
I begged for storms to come, loud and very frightening,
Gusts to strip the Earth, rain to flood the lands,
A storm to bring rebirth, until man understands.
I felt my anguish building, my anxiety would flood,
I watched the sun receding, I felt it could be good.
Wash away the cliff-sides, usher in some doom,
Feel the rising of the tides, ride in a monsoon.
Storm as if you know me, Thunder, say my name,
Come and set my world free, cry with me again.
Apocalypse, Ragnarök, Armageddon, cataclysm,
Speak now of the end times to this lonely growing prison.
Send to me the wind-sweeps, a torrential downpour to this land,
Speak to me of rivers, flowing over where I stand.

Praying for Clouds

Death

Stoneworld

These cracks that appear slowly,
Fissures right below me,
I see the passage of time,
Wrinkles forming lines,
A thousand passing ages,
Drifting across the pages,
The years that drifted by,
The breathing of the sky,
The Earth that wakes so slowly,
The ground has come to know me,
Here within the seams,
Crystal dust as dreams,
Shine brightly heated rock,
A key to time's unlock,
Aeons so cast away,
Years like just a day,
Cool as stone to gem,
Shined and polished again,

I'll shine in any light,
Perfect in your sight,
Rulers claim my worth,
Wealth not to disperse,
The treasure of my knowledge,
Come and pay me homage,
I've seen the Earth since birth,
I know its pain and worth,
I fear no mortal man,
It has its own great plan,
Hard and strong to grind,
Forever does unwind,
One day, you'll all be dust,
Crushed and lost to rust,
But here I'll still reside,
Shining in my pride.

Becoming Death

There's a fog across the land,
Black skin along my hands,
My fingernails grow dark,
My soul is surely marked,
I feel the force growing,
Around me time is slowing,
I can feel myself changing,
With every breath that I draw,
My soul is rearranging,
And I feel cold to my core,
Every garment that I wear,
Becomes hooded and black,
In the cold night beware,
Only gods push me back,

You have always walked beside,
You have been my only friend,
I feel your presence inside,
We'll be one before the end,
I felt you in the sunrise,
And in the changing seasons,
I looked deep into your eyes,
To find meaning and reasons,
You held me like a mother,
Loved me gently as your son,
I knew you as my brother,
In the times I never won,
Though I knew that you were there,
Like a father there to guide,
At first, I was so scared,
And I tried to run and hide,

I knew that you were there,
But not that you were me,
I felt you in the air,
And I saw your clarity,
Now that I have let you in,
I can feel you on my skin,
It grows ghostly pale,
The decay is getting stale,
There's a mist around my feet,
And a stillness on the streets,
I take every last breath
Usher living into death,
Some children can see me,
All shall learn my name,
I've come to set all free,
Life's forces shall be tamed,

All creatures and the old,

Flee from my scent,

And every tool that I hold,

Becomes crooked and bent,

I, bringer of strife,

Harvester with scythe,

Harbinger of doom,

Some say I come too soon,

The force around me spirals,

With bacteria and virus,

Death is all I will know,

I'll harvest your essence,

All fear my presence,

I will reap and I will sow.

The Reaper

Life brings us challenges and people to meet,
The hard-nose-grinds and stamping our feet,
Tossing and turning unable to sleep,
Breaking down and starting to weep.

We all have our problems, our tests and our troubles,
But you'll find some relief when the kettle bubbles.
It's the way that you deal with the problems you face,
That can make you a winner in this ruthless rat race.

Cherish the people who are there to stay,
Who'll help you make use of each passing day.
It's not who they are when times are good,
But how they react when dragged through mud.

You might struggle and fight, but you could just give in,
Life isn't a battle you can easily win.
The reaper will come and you've met your end,
And there's all that money you didn't spend.

You may be wrapped, in sudden fear,
When you find that your end is already here.
The tunnel is narrow and the end is bright,
You'll find no simple end to your plight.

As the light you seek is drawing near,
There is a solemn whisper in your ear.
You cannot go where I have been,
If you do not know what I have seen.

When face-to-face, the eye is your maker,
The generous giver and vengeful taker,
While moving towards a magnificent glow,
The Shadows behind will surely grow.

The Shadow of the Mountain

Walk in misty mountain hail,
Through windswept hidden vale,
The fog will roll across the land,
Black harvest and Death's hand.
In the shadow of the mountaintop,
Rising lands never stop,
Rolling hills forever on,
All who walk it lost and gone.
In the dark and dead of night,
The living have no sight,
When on that path and faced with fear,
Look east and north to here.

Topsy-Turvy World

When less is more and more is less,
If up is down it's all a mess
The roof's the floor and I'm no more,
My ego slides out through the door
If good were bad and harm was gentle,
If sanity's real then we're all mental,
If pain were nice or once was twice,
If freedom really had no price,
If money were free or us free from money,
If shit were food, its taste like honey
If once bitten twice shy, then now fallen can't fly
If angel's dust spread disease,
If politicians lived to please
If right was wrong or wrong was right,
Then we would never have to fight
If life was death and death was life,
We'd see a world that's free from strife

If all we love must fade away,
If all the light will turn to grey
If old was new and new was old,
This story's gone, already told
If gold turned black and clocks turned back,
The Earth would shatter and rocks crack
If tears would heal the fears I feel,
If all our hearts were cold as steel
If all our minds were dull as stone,
We'd never have to feel alone
If empty was full and we weren't empty,
If hate was love we all had plenty
If all the world weren't bent and curvy,
If all these things were topsy-turvy.

Ghost

You said you'd never want me,
You're the ghost that I can see,
You're there in shade at night,
You fade away in daylight.
You taunt me in the darkness,
You're wearing an ether dress,
You are all that I can see,
Will you ever set me free?
I look each way in daylight,
But the light is all too bright,
It hides your wisps and trails,
But the evening soon unveils.
I see your pale reflection,
Otherworldly imperfection,
The once too-human face,
Still there in some small trace.
You follow me in shadows,
It is death your body knows,
Your warmth is turned to chill,
A ghost that can't sit still.

Fire

Fire and Ash

Set my skin on fire
And my soul ablaze,
Burn me with desire,
Melt me in a haze.

Burn all that I am
And all that I'll be;
Return me to ash,
Please come set me free.

Which pieces will burn?
What left will remain?
What will the flame learn?
What will fire gain?

Mistress of the Flame

Fire loves to dance,
I see her beauty,
Light, heat, romance,
She fulfils her duty,
In mesmerising swirls,
She really excites me,
She flows and she twirls,
She will set me free.

Maybe I'll be burned,
That's the thrill I love,
She must be earned.
A light from up above,
The others have girls,
They are not as hot.
Her phoenix wing furls,
Sexier than the lot.

She crackles and sizzles,
She's smouldering and steaming,
She engulfs then fizzles,
Around it all streaming.
Some want to tame,
The wildness of her,
Never twice the same,
Lighting up the air.

My mistress is fire,
She has sexy flame,
Together on my pyre,
Then I'll learn her name?

Water & Fire

The heat of raging fire,
To burn is its desire,
Fuel, air and heat,
Melting as they meet.

Water sacred and pure,
Thirst's known cure,
Tranquil and so calm,
Protecting all from harm.

Cloaked in raging flame,
Soaked in ocean rain,
A meld of hot and cold,
The rise of hot steam,
A force to behold.

A battle at the seam,
Two forces set to meet,
Not meant to be at one,
Here they are so sweet.

The rage will soon be gone,
See the fires burn,
What secrets do I learn?
In her eyes waters pool,
Set to soothe and cool.

She sets my skin ablaze,
Extinguishes with her gaze,
Her aura is steaming,
Her light is gleaming.

The burning of the soul,
In her heat I drench,
Two opposites are whole,
In her I burn and quench.

Cataclysm

Bring the clouds and black the skies,
Block the sun that blinds the eyes,
Soak the ground so dry and scorched,
Fuel the fires and burn the torch,
Roll on thunder and lightning flash,
Fall in wonder and frightening crash,
Bring the rains assault the land,
Give me pain and free my mind,
Beckon doom and summon hell,
Sonic boom and storming swell,
Feel the gusts and cyclone rush,
Peeling winds and power's push,
The rain like bombs from other worlds,
Drench my bones, stampede the herds,
Falling drops and swelling flood,
All is stopped where fear is stood,

The ground is gone, the earth cracks,
The end is nigh, the sky attacks,
Free me now from earthly prison,
Destroy the world in cataclysm,
Split all atoms and rip apart,
Cut down forests and take the heart,
Feel the rage that has been freed,
Tear the land and salt the seeds,
Rip up life and all plantations,
Peel the earth, destroy foundations,
Break the map and kill the path,
Desire reveals the height of wrath,
Let land bleed and the rivers blacken,
Shattered creed, release the kraken,
For gods we suffer, we are man,
Return to nothing, fate's last plan.

Rise

Like a corpse from the dust,
Or a tornado with the gust,
Like a volcano from the ground,
With a dull earthquake sound,
I'll grow and I'll erupt,
I'll show what is corrupt,
Like a swallow in the morning,
Or the red sun dawning,
Like a chick from an egg,
Or the first pint from a keg,
I will soar and I will rise,
Can you see it in my eyes?
Like a phoenix from the ash,
I will turn it all to glass,
Like a living, soaring flame,
I will burn it all the same,

The plant that will not live,
Or a ghost that won't forgive,
Like a legend in a story,
Or a climbing morning glory,
I will reach for untold highs,
I believe that I will rise,
Like a tree from dusty bones,
Or a church from quarried stones,
Like a pharaoh from a tomb,
Or a child from mother's womb,
There is no task too big in size,
I will conquer and I will rise.

Angels & Demons

Veiled Nightmares & Ethereal Dreams

The night holds secrets deep within,
The depths of darkness and under skin,
The hold it has on earth and sky,
As I sit alone and wonder why,
I dream in day and through the night,
Settling fears and gaining sights,
The veil that hides the truth from me,
Behind the nightmares I can see,
The Angel saved my heart and soul,
The Goddess returned what once she stole,
The night conspired to swallow whole,
When sunlight ripped and tore the hole,
The veiled nightmare was all I knew,
The only freedom that helped me through,
When I saw a soul lost in the ether,
Calling to me, the long-lost sleeper,
The shapes of wisps and forces grew,
The heavens called and sang of you,
My heart and mind both broke in two,
My soul just left to follow you,
The nightly sleep brought back your face,
You came to me then left no trace,

A man wept of dreaming night and day,
Tossing and turning, drifting away,
He sees the light so lost to him,
The dreams and nightmares making dim,
Crash through fire and burning flames,
The helpful goddess and forgotten name,
Here to see what can be tamed,
Outside of self and without shame,
The veil flutters in otherworldly winds,
The nightmare holds and branded singe,
The dream awakens and tears his wings,
The Angel laughs all the while she sings,
Heaven sent and hell-bound soul,
The light you knew and truth you stole,
Despair has carved for you a role,
Set a path and shown the goal,
But when the light and smile turn cold,
And I found no friend here to behold,
I turned away from the life you showed,
Paying back the cost and what I owed.

The Nameless Demon

The wind and fear are forming a typhoon,
The sound I hear is pain here all too soon,
The thing that feeds the nerves inside my soul,
Resounding with the weeds to swallow whole.
The vortex of my raging anger rotates,
Inside the hex of my cursed lover's fates,
The swirling of my demon takes its form,
The grey and blackened clouds create a storm.
The winds echo the pain that holds my heart,
The sins of all my past draws solemn art,
The water cuts right through me, drenching bone,
My skin just shuts me in, I'm so alone.
Gust for me the torrent of my torment,
Trust this plea, abhorrently ferment,
Let the skies bring nought for me this night,
Jet-black eyes, the demon here to fight.

All the tools that could have helped me win,
Are lost and torn asunder now within,
Tail and vicious claws made of my dreams,
Torn amongst the tapestry's tattered seams.
Will the demon have his day at last?
Has this moment's setting long been cast?
Did I write my name in tainted blood,
The seal amongst the doorway where it stood?
As lightning cracks the sky and I face my doom,
There's only one last thought amongst the gloom,
Once I was a young boy who had a chance,
Once the world held wonder and romance.
So face me as you rip from other realm,
Here I am, driving my faults, I'm at the helm,
If this has come to be my final fight,
I won't lie down and quietly drift from sight.

The eyes you wear of darkness that you stole,
Cannot fight the disparity that made me whole,
If darkness is the force from whence you came,
If evil is what gave you your foul name,
If the wielding of this terror is what made me,
Then maybe it's this fight could set me free,
No yearning for the light here down below,
The things that live in darkness will help me grow.
As if amongst the dirty, dark and rust,
Ashes of ages, dust of my mistrust,
I'll rise with all the tools I've made down here,
Stricken to this sombre, looming fear.
The things that once shone brightly in the light,
Are all lost down here with me in the night,
This may be your home, your battleground,
But I hear the living voice call all around.

Darkness is my friend, this can be my home,
Accept it and I'll never feel alone,
So I'll rise on wings of darkness and black fire,
A meld of terrible things and deep desire,
Up into the skies where the stars still shine,
Amongst the black of night where lovers pine,
I'll write a story of loss and leave it here,
Of a dance of demon and man in stratosphere.
I'll leave your stricken carcass there to rot,
Carrion for the vultures to be forgot,
Demon, don't defile me, I'm evil's son,
You entered a battle that could not be won,
Here I fell in love with night's abyss,
Lusted for her twisted, deathly kiss.

Angel Image

I made you in my image,
Now you're shaping me in yours,
I coloured all your plumage,
While I was bleeding from pores.

My deaf ears they heard nothing,
Which death's voice did not describe,
My hands were so unstopping,
They moved quickly to inscribe.

My blood stained you deeply red,
But you drew me closer in,
The splatter fell from my head,
As your love I felt within.

Oh, Angel, how you saved me,
You guided me through the night,
Angel, how you set me free,
Bathed me gently in your light.

You swiftly lifted my fears,
As you slowly eased my pain,
Healing softly with your tears,
As you pleased my lonely brain.

You said I could discover,
How to mend my broken soul,
You said I could recover,
That I too could become whole.

Your feathers, oh so soothing,
They protect me from it all,
Together we are moving,
Now with you I'll never fall.

Night with an Angel

She came in the night,
Wondrous in flight,
Floating through air,
Golden-white hair,
Perfect skin pigment,
She must be a figment,
She's inside my brain,
Erasing my pain,
Caressing my soul,
And making me whole,
She eases my stings,
I'm folded in wings,
The silk of her skin,
Is drawing me in,
She helps me to see,
She's setting me free,

I feel I could weep,
I must be asleep,
Together we grow,
We both let go,
So light in my clutch,
Responding to touch,
Our tangling muffled,
Her feathers ruffled,
We lay together,
Please stay forever,
But soon it is done,
And up comes the sun,
Winds blow, I mutter,
I hear a flutter
I cry and I call,
At shadows on walls.

The Other Side

Through the withered veil,
Down the spiral trail,
On this other side,
Nowhere here to hide,
Through the looking glass,
A world beyond mass,
Here do I exist?
Does myself persist?
Here asking for power,
From the angel tower,
Mortality long behind,
What truth will I find?
Destroying all the odds,
Power from the gods.
The secrets of us all,
Beyond the parting wall,

This life's true meaning,

My consciousness convening,

The truth of wonder,

Tears me now asunder,

From my body torn,

My flesh soon reborn,

Free from my reality,

Beyond my own mortality,

Free from my flesh,

Can I start afresh?

Beyond the human realm

Driving at the helm,

I offer no resistance,

Feel power of existence,

Here now, I forage,

Eating fruit of knowledge.

Rebirth

The Spring Forge

When the sun beats the hedgerows and rises anew,
When the fields glitter brightly in fresh morning dew,
When the spring calls to heaven and man ploughs the earth,
Will I break from my skin as my soul is rebirthed?
Rise with these feelings and live within love,
Call up to the skies, gods and angels above,
Bring me my heart now and the one with the key,
Loosen these shackles I am set to be free,
The sapphire skies and the emerald-green trees,
Flow soundly right through as they blow with an ease.

The orange and red of the new dawning sun,
It says so many things as the morning is won.
As the clouds reflect back the darkness I felt,
I feel I have found peace, in the aroma I smelt,
Under their canopy of white it glows red,
Like the fires of hell and the self that I shed,
In fires so forged and in fire I live,
I will never tire, I will work and I'll give,
The iron in my blood and the carbon of my frame,
Will lead me to good and can free me from shame.

So when the songbirds are singing and the summer is here,
I will feel I deserve you as I let go my fear,
When the light showers fall and drizzle soaks through,
Will the cold steel feel warm as I draw into you?
Can the dull metal sharpen and the furnace feel full,
Cold surfaces polish an edge from that lull,
With each hammer blow and the chime of the anvil?
With every soak in the water I impart some will,
When my fingers grow pained and my hands know each blow.
Will the forge without malice be all that I know?

The fuel fills the furnace and the fires rage on,
The ringing of iron and steel is my song,
Sing me to life to the new self I will craft,
More subtly sharp and acutely apt.
Feel the parts of my new self and the ones I've forsook,
Destiny from the shelf with the hope that I took,
When the smithing is over and the insignias take hold,
Enchanting and shining, gilded in finest gold,
My rebirth will be done my new life will take form,
As I join hands with you and my heart feels so warm.

The Hands of the People

Let the rain fall across these hills,
And wash away our sins,
Let the skies open on these lands,
and clean our dirty hands.

See the children poor and cold,
Drink full of Nature's bosom,
Let the wind's voice be told,
It cries aloud for them.

Let the hungry bunker down,
Abandoned by their kin,
See the leaves turn red and brown,
At the whitening of the skin.

The politicians argue and bicker,
As the darkness grows thicker,
Watch the suffering of the weak,
As hope turns thin and bleak.

Watch the skies grow grey and dark,
See autumn make its mark,
The rain will wash upon these hills,
But will it take their sins?

See the rich hoard their gains,
While farmers store their grains,
Watch the rise of the wealthy,
Their children spoilt and healthy.

See disparity all around,
As the lost sleep wet upon the ground,
Watch the land betray its people,
As rain soaks church and wind sweeps steeple.

Hear the ringing of the bells,
Could capitalism be felled?
A hungry, starving tool of profit,
Somehow we have to stop it.

The rain will pour across these lands,
We could wash blood from our hands,
We could stand by all our kin,
Together we could win.

Like the rain we have to fall,
We could stand and fight,
Together we could share it all,
We could claim that right.

Soon the rain will wash our land,
It will cover up their greed,
Wouldn't it be very grand,
If we could sow the seed?

Feel the coming of the weather,
Feel the rolling change within,
The shrill shiver for our kin,
Know that we could stand together.

Hello

Hello to the darkness,
The morning cold and dew,
Hello to the coldness,
The silence running through.
Hello to the winds
That call to me again,
Hello, angel wings
That blow away my pain.

Goodbye to the torrent
That soaked into my bones,
Torn inside that current
So scared I was alone.
Hello to the people,
I'm glad you all are here,
Hanging bell on steeple,
Ring it loud and clear.

Goodbye to my torment,
I grew within your grasp,
Goodbye to the moments,
The ones I couldn't clasp.
Farewell to the dreams,
The ones I must forget,
Tearing at the seams,
The fabric of regret.

I'll wave goodbye to sorrow,
And hello to new friends,
The embrace of tomorrow,
And the promise that it lends.
So hello, thoughts and feelings,
That move to feed my soul
And hello to the healing,
I'm ready to be whole.

Glastonbury

Come and pop your cherry,
Your first Glastonbury,
Get caked in mud and shite,
Stay up on drugs all night.
Fall on tents and strangers,
In the land of Middle Earth,
Face the untold dangers,
In the place of your rebirth.
Your quest is so immense,
The booze may yet run out,
Don't piss on the fence,
Or the green police will shout,
I hope your boots are good,
And your wellies high and warm,
This land is prone to flood,
The seagulls known to swarm.

Don't forget your tent poles,
Remember your big coat,
Eat stale sausage rolls,
Use an airbed for a boat.
There will be many issues,
The mud may squelch and ooze,
You'll need wipes and tissues
When you venture to the loos,
Where bloody tampons sail,
And the smell will hit you hard,
Where many squatters fail,
Miss the target by a yard.
The ride will all be worth it,
The journey home so rough,
If the headlines play their hits,
'Til we've all had enough!

Different

Tomorrow, I'll be different because yesterday was tough,
Stay a final hour, things have gotten rough.
Now the day grows late; our time has flowed away,
We reach this sorry state; we don't know what to say.
Everywhere I look I am reminded of a dream,
Our time together, our lack of luck, it makes me wanna scream.
The hand that held so gently and the voice that soothed my soul,
I loved you so intently, your heart has played its role.
I remember how you smelled and how you touched my heart,
Feel how I'd do it different, if I could have another start.

So tomorrow, I'll be dealing with the traumas of the past,
Lonely and revealing as they open me at last.
They'll see a love for you that's there, lost among the pain,
They'll know of how I long for you and wish for you again.

They'll see my chances slipped from me and
know that I'm too late,
They'll know I wonder if our time could have instead been great.
But in my heart and in my soul a seed has sprouted roots,
Up into my mind and through my dreams its power shoots.
The magic you awoke in me flows powerful and real,
It flows on through my veins and on my skin as I am healed,
Your beating heart holds power
and your touch feels silky smooth,
The air is glowing lightly as this power's might is proved.

So tomorrow will be different because I am changed for good,
I tried with all my might and now my path is understood.

Stillness & Silence

Stillness and silence, silence and stillness,
No room for violence, no cure for illness,
It moves in me as it fills the space,
Everything and everywhere, leaving ghostly trace.
I feel its mark around me, moving through me, marking time,
It lies between the syllables and at the end of every rhyme.
The tip of my tongue stunned, feels the need to break its hold,
To speak and to be listened to, see what words unfold.
But in the summer nightly breeze, the air still sings to me,
The birds are calling loudly and the trees are blowing free,
Around me and within me there's a calm before a storm,
A sudden altercation as I seek for strength and form,
Each thing in life must have a place, a use for which it is,
Find it and then fuse with it, watch reactions boil and fizz.

Silence lives in all the things, the earth holds fast its name,
It keeps it hidden deep below the rocks that form its frame,
The stillness of a tranquil pond the water clear and pure,
Look deep into the depths,
through your reflection see much more.
The time has flowed around me, and my mind and soul are old,
I've been whipped by life so mightily my skin is scarred and bold,
The lines that make my face this way are adding to my years,
Who is this man who looks at me, the one who holds these fears?
So shape me in this moment, my attention held for now,
Shake me from my torments, let these feelings show me how,
I'll turn this stillness inwards and use it to find a way,
I'll forge this silent wilfulness to build a better day.

Short Poems

Night Knife

The sharpest cold, the longest night,
The depths of loneliness,
To pain behold and feel this fright
Sat in this sordid mess.

The night surrounds and steals my air,
Suppressing all I love,
It's all around, it's everywhere,
Below and all above.

The sharpest blade, the thinnest needle,
The keenest cutting edge,
My bed is made, I know the bleeding
Will flow in oozing dredge.

So all in all, I have my pain,
No light to guide my way,
The pain is filling me again
Between words I couldn't say.

So in this night and through this dark,
The edge of an abyss,
And in my sights I leave a mark
As I see what's left of this.

The night has seeped into my skin,
The muscle and the sinew,
The blade has cut me bleeding through
This feeling all I knew.

Punching God

Oh, to punch the face of God
And take the bastard's golden rod,
The power that he has abused,
Would be much better used,
As the old god's power faltered,
A new world formed and altered,
I'd usher in a golden age,
And rewrite every page.

Fairies And Rainbows

I've gone off the grid chasing leprechauns and rainbows,
There might not be a pot of gold,
But if I catch a fairy on the wind, I'll ask her for a wish,
I'll wish for her to sail away with me, to distant horizons,
Where the sun never sets and dreams never die,
Where fairy tales come true and where people never lie,
I'll chase the sun across the sky
faster than the turning of the world,
And time itself will cease to flow,
And there, on the crest of that horizon,
I'll bathe in her glow.

Feather

I saw a feather dancing nimbly on the wind,
The joy I felt as I watched it made my heart sing.
The sunlight shone off the feather, and its radiance was bright,
So utterly brilliant, such a welcome delight.
The feather holds my wishes in each grain and line,
Hopes that can be and dreams to be mine.
Maybe I am as that feather, floating on a breeze,
From wind to wind as if it comes with ease.
I use each gust hoping to rise above,
Wishing to trust and reach ecstatic love,
To find the zenith and reach eternal bliss.
Alas, I reach the nadir and succumb to fear,
Fearing that I will return stricken to the ground,
Where my abject failure won't even make a sound.

The Tide of the Moment

When it all starts fading and you know it's gone too soon,

The dreams will be evading as the silence loudly booms,

Sonic waves around you as it fills the empty rooms,

The walls they ask for something, doorways speak of doom,

Trapped inside this feeling, something anxious deep inside,

We gave up the search for meaning, we are happy to reside,

Here stuck with this moment, there is nowhere left to hide,

Feel the waves your mind creates through this ever-rising tide.

So you let go in the flow and feel it washing over you,

Swept away to nowhere but you've nothing else to do,

So turbulent the currents, so powerful and new,

This is the only thing you think that really could be true.

Wishing Well

Wish upon a wishing well,
Story for the fish to tell,
Bring me joy now with your spell,
Throw the penny down to hell.

Give me just another wish,
Listen for another splish,
To the water bucket miss,
Penny for another kiss.

Wishing on a wishing well,
Down into the magic fell,
Bring another soul to sell,
Fear in me your power quell.

All my pennies you to take,
Hear my dreams for my own sake,
Worlds will form and I'll remake,
Power unto me awake.

Depression

Shadow Self

The still, tranquil surface of the water contrasts the storm of my raging mind; I look through the surface and see the reflection of all my hopes and dreams, so far away it seems as it gleams back at me. I can see but I cannot reach, and every time I touch the water, I become wet as it ripples; the ripples fan out and may yet become waves. How do I make it through to the other side? Here, I feel trapped; I am but a boy among men, a child among women. I am lost amongst the saved and missing around the found. I am a soul among soulless, wicked among valiant and evil among the gallant.

If only I could break the surface…

My reflection looks back, and I am bare to his inspection. Like me but not me, he taunts slyly, asking so many questions: are you happy? are you loved? are you…you? I recoil at the question as I ask myself who I am and who I want to be. The very suggestion makes me reach out a hand and splash the reflection away, but here I know, under this inspection, and with time, I can find my true self.

Depression

Have you ever been depressed?
I have, I'll confess.
Have you ever fought your mind?
All the time.

Have you ever watched your love
Bang their head on the wall,
Or witnessed your best friend's psychotic fall?
Have you ever been at war with your own mind?
Have you ever called the crisis line to find
That there is no help anywhere?

So go, be alone, and you'd better be scared.
They don't hear your voices, and you'll never be heard.
Trapped and alone, you scream at the walls,
But nobody ever answers your calls.
Locked in your world, your own cataclysm,
Where is the key to this infinite prison?

Have you ever been scared to be on your own?
Felt trapped as you sit all alone in your home?
Well, I have been up, and I have been down.
I'm no king, and there won't be a crown.

But I am still here, despite all my fear,
Though one day I might disappear.

For now, let me try to open some eyes.
Please answer the pleas and cries.
I've hated life. And I've begged for death.
I've felt pain drawing with every breath.
Am I just a coward? Who stands here today?
Just a failure with too much to say?

The path has been hard, the road has been long,
The nights cold when I wasn't strong.
I've faced myself, and I've learnt the truth,
In the castoffs of my misspent youth.
The bonds that we make, the promise I took,
Keeps me here; it's my anchor, my hook.

So I'll forge ahead, and I'll make my way,
Find the beauty that hides in the day.
But for those who cry and those who are broken,
It's about time these words were spoken.

Broken Children

We are the children of broken children,
The lost among the lost.
We are the ones whose problems kill them,
The cold between the frost.
We are the meaning between the letters,
The hurt behind the song,
Those who needed better,
Those who feel so wrong.

We are the anguish in every break-up,
The tear in every eye,
The vanity behind make-up,
The reason babies cry.
We are the life that's gone too early,
The friendship lost and broken,
The cycle passing yearly,
The words kept, never spoken.

The call for help from nowhere,
The response it will not come,
The man who should've loved her,
The fading, setting the sun.

I am the man whose dreams have faded,
Before they ever had a chance,
The one whose heart is jaded,
A failure at romance.
I am the empty side of all beds,
The frost beneath the sheets.
I am the problems in my head,
The sum of my defeats.

I am the son my father made me,
The one he couldn't love.
I am the one set to be free,
My sins to carry above.

Echoes Of The Past

We don't talk anymore and your voice is no longer there,
There's nothing in my ear and the whispers don't care.
The noise you once gifted me and the regular vibrations,
Are just echoes of the past now and forgotten to the ages.
The voice that once lifted me reverberates right through,
The sound just gyrates; it can't escape too.
The joy it once resembled makes me tremble as I think,
It's the deafening sound of golden brown or pink.
I hear a distant rumbling and its mumbling in your voice –
Sometimes I even stop or turn; and for a moment I rejoice.

But we don't talk anymore and I never see your face,
The sound that is so haunting like a ghost's hanging trace.
The air pings nothings like a distant ringing,
The winds speak to me as if they're quietly singing,
Bringing me news of your faraway dreams,
Speaking your views along tentative seams.

Sometimes it paints a picture, a memory of your face;
It's something unnerving that I never can trace.
It hovers a moment and then hangs in the air,
As I look into the light, it fades in the glare.

But though we are done talking, I still speak in distant ways,
Responding to your messages along the air's connecting lays,
Mutters of our journeys, witty marks are quipped,
The butterfly flutters causing winds to be whipped.
The atmosphere moves with the sound of our chat;
Sometimes I even think that I know where you're at –
Lost among the energy that flows and moves,
Blowing with the wind and the power it proves.
The distant memory of your echoing sound,
That speaks through the air and talks from the ground,
The constant shaking of a forgotten echo,
That says with your voice, it's time to let go,
Talking through the air with words across the sky,
It's time to move on now, so let's say goodbye.

Understanding Pain

I was never the tallest, the quickest or strongest,
Though I was sometimes funny and strange.
I would sometimes smile broadly or laugh the longest,
Showing lines that scream years beyond age.
Under my skin and inside my mind,
There's a battle that you couldn't know,
Once a thought to go back or an urge to rewind,
Before this pain had started to grow.
Never the one to be best or be worst,
Just an average man before you,
Repeating these lines as though they're rehearsed,
With this pen I can seek what is true.
But what of these torments, these traumas I feel?
If I stop, will they swallow me whole?
The years they have taken, the fear in me wakens,
The aeons and ages they stole.

But I do have one skill from the doors of despair,
One thing if you listen to the rain:
I've travelled alone, a long way if you will,
And I have gained understanding of pain.
The way it takes your whole body, it sits in your throat,
affecting everything said and wrote,
Takes over your life and over your dreams,
It is all that you've heard and spoke.
So when pain comes a-calling, and you feel you are falling,
I'll be there with fast food and affection.
We won't disappear we can conquer this fear,
Tackle this growing infection.

Crumble

The leaves tumble and fall in the darkness; I breathe into my mess. How many have crumbled? Each one is a memory of a world, a moment, a hope or a wish, a dream that died or a lover's final kiss. They hold the memories of hope as they pass, the boundary between life and death, summer and autumn, hope and despair. They echo my heart and the sentiment that lies in me.

Will they crumble to dust as we forget the world that was, all the moments that we seized in the light summer's day, when the red grape wine wet our lips and we danced under the watchful gaze of the bright warm sun, the moments of fun and friendship, of love and joy that warmed us to our hearts?

The trees grew with us as their blossoms bloomed with the bright spark of life; the leaves sprouted as the branches held them and nurtured them in their moment between boundaries. In that moment, I found me, and I stood to address myself. I connected with the life cycle and the synergy I felt, the flow of their energy and their connection with the Earth as I awaited my rebirth.

I watch the parts of me I lost, and I kick them as I see them scatter amongst the curled and dried-up leaves. As the pieces of me I cast away crumble and cross the boundary to the next plain, finally I am me, and I feel whole as I acknowledge my soul again. That world already seems so far away as I look up at the empty branches and remember all those wasted chances. I've had plenty, but I accept that I can waste no more energy on what is gone as I pierce through the darkness and know that I am ready to move on.

Sun

Sun

Let me trace the sun across the ever-moving skies,
I'll hook the moon and stars and keep them only for my eyes.
Let me ask the moon, just once, why it runs from the sun;
Let me call a star to Earth and fate can be undone.
The equinox and solstice form a cycle to the east;
The sun will rise in newer skies, a mythic man or beast.
Let it turn and let it burn, ice ages fade to past;
Let the winter sun be warm and let the thawing last.

Will the stars please draw for me a map to guide my way?
The path that has been worn for me has trapped me in the day.
So can I have sunglasses and a hat to hide my face?
Can I dress as black as night until my path is traced?
Heroes live amongst the stars and poets among words;
I wonder which bear deeper scars torn looking at the birds.
Born under a Libra sign, the balance must be sought,
Torn in wonder from divine one who won't be bought.

Zodiacs and heroes choose their tools to fight for fate,
So if I must find balance, then I hope I'm not too late.
So let me balance all my sins against the weight of what I seek,
This could be my chance to fly on wings to higher peaks.
So send me on a journey, fly me round the stars;
Send me on a spaceship built by aliens on Mars.

When I travel onwards, out through the space and time,
To find some of the fire that burns white and so sublime,
I'll wonder all the stories that are told about our sun,
I'll sit and tell it jokes, I'll poke around and have some fun.
I'll ask it when its light will fade
and when my soul will be released,
I'll tell it what I know of shade
and how I'll find my peace.

Aging Sun

There's a wry and lonely smile,
Across the edges of my aging face.
It's like the widening grin of the setting sun,
The dull glow which leaves me yearning,
As I watch the fading of another day,
The loss of which leaves me longing.

As the time just drifts away,
Frightened by the impending dark,
The night will come, and I will become,
The creature of the night that is feared,
The wretched monster so revered,
Where none shall see my true face,
Or look upon the beauty that has faded.

As I morph into my new self,
I try to shed the skin of what was before,
But I see a reflection shining in the sky,
Captivated by the beauty I see once more.
I think about the choice I made and wish,
Oh, how I wish that I had remained pure.

The face that I discarded and disregarded is gone,
Like the day that is beyond my grasp,
Lost and forgotten as with my new face I cry,
I ball and scream and begin to rasp.
But I know whatever the cost, it is lost,
Beyond all recognition at last,
As I recognise that I, am truly jaded.

The Precipice

On the precipice between dark and light,
I've waited and waited, I've sat here all night.
The darkness caresses and envelopes me so;
My eyes and my senses found inner a glow.
On the edge of the horizon, there'll soon be a sight,
I'll see the sun risin'; I'll feel it shine bright.
Behind me rain clouds still feed to this land;
In front, it is dry as I move air with my hand.
There are so many places, but right here I stand,
Between all the spaces, beneath what is grand.
I don't want to go backwards, but forwards is far,
So I'm staying right here; I can see where we are.
The sky sees a flash, and it's lit by a star;
It helps me to see, penetrating the dark.
I'll make a wish for my dreams of tomorrow,
But right now, it seems I've no future to follow.
Yesterday's hopes are now so far away,
So here I am, waiting, between night and day.

Happiness

I'm not sure how to feel or if it's even right.
My soul begins to heal; I am bathed in healing light.
Happiness never taught me much;
it hasn't made me who I am,
Though it fills me at your every touch
and when I hold your hand.

Happiness never wrote sombre words of deep decay,
Though it was spoke among the birds and hiding in the day.
It never wrote a masterpiece or became a famous bard;
Because it was never palpable, it was hiding; it was hard.

But though it didn't do these things,
it taught me something good:
It taught me how to love and live
and chase the dreams I should.
I caught it in the small things,
in your smile and on your lips;
It avoids the lords and rich kings
like the wiggle of your hips.

It's there among the sunbeams and shining in your hair,

With your voice, its name gleams; I can finally see it there.

In your arms, I know I've found my one and only home;

With you, I can believe that I don't have to die alone.

So happiness can give me love; love can bring me joy –

All the things I've longed for and I hoped I could enjoy,

All the pain I so revered as in night I disappeared,

All the things I've feared since this darkness appeared.

But this must be the feeling that so many feel sometimes,

To be captured and revealing and written here in rhymes.

Around me, walls are shattered

like a pick through clear white ice.

The cold veil breaks and cuts me,

but this feeling's oh so nice.

I raise my head to look at you,

and as I do, I know what comes.

Your soul to me is humming like a thousand burning suns.

I look into the dawn light you emit as though you know,

I fall beneath this onslaught lost forever in your glow.

One I Loved

I loved you when the land was cold
And the winds blew strong with ice.
Your healing love was there to hold,
You made me feel so nice.
I found you when the leaves were red
And the land was barren and bare.
I remember how you warmed my bed
And the passionate pink of your hair.
I felt you as the sheets were warmed
And the caring silk of your skin.
I felt my soul as it reformed
And the healing change within.
I loved you when the nights were long
And the sun hid low in the sky.
I felt that I had become strong,
That we could soar so high.
I saw green spring from the ground
And was filled with humble awe.
I felt the air warm all around
And the strength of summer thaw.

But some things can never last
And the sun can burn too hot.
The fire's passion furnace blast
On the land that ice forgot.
I lost you as my heart broke
And the land grew cold again.
So many things unspoken
As they flooded through my brain.
I missed you when the rains fell,
And the clouds came at my call.
I kissed you in the storm's swell,
In the autumn shower's fall.
I know you in my heart still;
You live on inside my soul.
There's a space that only you fill,
Where your memory plays a role.

Other

Figments

There are figments that find me and creatures of light,
There are those who I see, they go bump in the night.
There are demons and ghouls and golems of stone,
They break all the rules, they cry and they moan.
There are goblins and orcs and things from all walks,
There are gremlins and bunyips and puddles that talk.
There are angels and spirits and things in my mind,
There are ghosts and fairies and gods that I find.
There are tremors and shakes and mirrors that speak,
They quake and they watch me, the walls loudly creak.
They are hiding in cupboards and under my bed,
They are inside my mind and affecting my head.
There are those in my thoughts and those in my dreams,
There are some I have caught and some that have screams.
There are monsters and trolls and harpies so real,
They claw and they tear and they offer me deals.
Leprechauns, devils and servants of fate,
Wood-nymphs to love me and divas that hate.
I run and I cry but I cannot hide,
They're inside my soul and inside my mind.

Painting By Numbers

Please colour me in,
Before I fade,
Paint my skin,
Pick any shade,
Paint me by numbers,
Colour me with words,
Each stroke encumbers,
Parts me in thirds.

I'm brighter than white,
And darker than black,
Glow like a sprite,
My skin may crack,
Deeper than blue,
More shiny than gold,
Bathed in a hue,
The colour grows bold.

When orange I rage,
When red beware,
On the white page,
As if stuck there,
When in yellow,
I remain calm,
Soothed and mellow,
Like a relaxing palm.

When in bright green,
I blend in the bush,
Part of the scene,
Painted with tender brush,
Soon I'll break free,
As colours sink in.

Looking hot in pink,
Your inks in my skin,
Flowing through me,
The spectrum of colour,
Setting me free,
And making me fuller.

Part 2

Paint my soul red,
And orange with fire,
Clouds for my head,
Strung together with wire.

Paint my heart black,
A lump of dark matter,
The feeling's come back,
It beats with a clatter.

Paint my feet brown,
As if covered in mud,
Draw me down
Please, if you could.

Draw an outline,
Fill in the surround,
I might be fine
In the background.

No need to be clear
As long as I'm there,
Somewhere quite near,
Drawn in the air.

Pinocchio

The world is a charred mess of rusty metal,
We've cut our way in and plucked off the petal,
A searing mad mess of crumpled plastic,
Many live in fear and sadness, isn't it fantastic?
But oh, how our cities are so big and so grand,
This world has been shaped, but by whose hand?

What is it for, and does it have true meaning?
Is there beauty in a skyscraper's gleaming?
They stand as testament to the power of man,
In our destruction's wake we build what we can,
Into everything; pure man always delves,
Following the path we carve for ourselves.

Some throw away knowledge and abandon free thinking,
No need to forage or be messy and stinking,
In a clean, composed and unified state,
Slaves to money and unjust hate,
You were tainted by man just like all things,
You're a wooden puppet but you have no strings.

Such a job they did there's no need to pull,
You're a trained sheep; you'll hand them your wool.
No working in secret, your masters are on show,
There's no point in hiding as the puppeteers know,
Their tricks are so powerful, although some may see,
Struggling is futile because you'll never be free.

A Dream of Flight

Forever in a transitional phase, watching the world go by,
Making the most of all my days, attempting to learn to fly,
With feathers and glue and a couple of sticks,
I'll get up in the air,
With a bit of luck and some clever tricks,
surely I'll make it there.

I'll run, I'll jump, I'll flap and I'll flay, maybe I'll even cluck,
I tried with boards to make a runway, if only that's all it took.
Maybe I'll make it there someday,
or maybe I'm wasting my time,
Maybe men just aren't meant to fly,
maybe I should just climb.

Surely one day it will come true, surely one day I'll win,
I'll keep on trying until I break through,
I don't know how to give in.

What if I was meant to stay beneath the big blue sky?
What if I am meant to say, "I'll sit and wonder why."

So maybe I should sit and look as all the planes go by.
Maybe I'll use a rope and hook to pull me through the sky.
Maybe men just aren't allowed to feel those winds and airs,
To reach the clouds; maybe I should build a set of stairs.

Maybe I will make it soon up to a cloud with the birds,
When I'm up there, I'll soar and zoom;
I'll remember these few words.
I'll remember the notion I had to fly,
so I sat and wrote it out,
I'll glide through air, poetry in motion,
I'll laugh and play and shout.

Broken

I remember when I met you in the darkest of nights,
I still feel the way you saved me – it was love at first sight,
I felt your smile as it warmed through me,
And your eyes said be free,
So I tried to stay by your side,
But you stole all my pride,
The skies are hollow above,
But let me follow your love,
I feel broken, my soul's beaten, and my heart has been used,
We've not spoken, I've not eaten, to this pain I am fused,
So bruise my body, break my soul,
And keep the heart that you stole,
Shake my mind inside its case,
And feel the pain on my face,
For tonight I'll lie with you, and I'll speak only of joy.
When you feel me and you touch me – I love being your toy,
So use me just as you please, just don't leave me all alone,
If I call and I text you, will you answer your phone?

Oh, tomorrow would you miss me would you see me again?
In my sorrow you kissed me, now you live in my brain.
So don't leave me as you found me, baby, broken is fine,
All the people I meet will know for you I still pine.
I loved you just for a moment, but now that moment is gone,
For a second in a lifetime, maybe you felt like the one.
So leave me broken, alone, and take all I have left,
I hope it helps you to make it – I won't call it theft.
Go with these words and all these things I can gift,
Fly away with the birds and with your wings as a lift.
In the south they will love you, and the air will be clean,
With blue skies above you, you won't have to be mean.
I'll remember how you loved me, how you used me so,
I'll be glad you are free and hope that you found your glow.

Dream With Me

Dream with me in pastures new,
in sunlit vales and morning dew,
Shine with me as grass glows white,
when the sun is rising from endless night,
Lie with me between trees so green
as mountains rise and we paint the scene,
Play with me burning midnight oil,
when our skin is hot and the day recoils.

In times of joy and moments to come,
Forever in love beneath endless sun,
When time stands still and hearts beat together,
we can build a connection that will never sever,
Winds of change will blow around,
the lands will speak all their sounds,
Forests and crops will rise and fall in the ground,
and we'll find a cycle that never stops,
Beneath stars that twinkle so far away,
amongst the words we just couldn't say,
As the diamonds sprinkle their shining light,
we can make them our heart's favoured sight.

Do they live, do they die, could we reach out and touch
them, can we rise upon wings to that sky?

Amongst darkness and blackness and bleakness we dream,
in each other's arms like we've always been,
Hanging in hammocks, relaxing in tents,
the song of the summer still knocks,
Play me a symphony, an orchestral song,
of the love that we've felt for so long.
Shape me and guide me, my rose-coloured dreams,
as the pathways before us grow strong,
The sweet smells of summer and the taste of our cider
brings feelings of safety and home.

And here as we're dreaming, the spirits are scheming,
and I know that we're never alone,
So breathe with me, live with me, love with me now,
let the forces around show us how.
Let the calmness surround us and this feeling of oneness,
and the song of the mountains be loud,
As we drift into dreams of our lives and each other
and we know that we're lovers for life,
Let the sweet mountain air and our thoughts be aware
that our dreams and our love fills the air.

Hearts of War

Thump, thump, thump
Go the drums of war,
Bringing something more.
The skin that vibrates,
The ground duly shakes,
With the sound of feet,
And every dull beat,
My head is due rest,
I lean on your chest
Ba-bump, ba-bump, ba-bump,
And your heart shakes,
My eardrum breaks
The pumping of blood,
The rush and flood,
The flow of force,
Your mortal source,
The sound soothes,
Its music grooves,

Pump, pump, pump,
I listen to your sound,
I ignore the surround,
Beating on my drum,
Red with setting sun,
The sound in my ear,
The pound speaks fear,
Every separate beat,
Warns of my defeat,
Bang, Bang, Bang
The drums unrelenting,
My fight unrepenting,
The battle draws sunrise,
And fear I will disguise,
So much could be lost,
I ignore the cost,
I stand, I am to fight,
In dawn's morning light.

The Dream in my Nightmares

At night amongst the dark I dream,
In the dead of black I scheme,
In the depths of fragile broken mind,
What worlds and folds to find.
The bright face that haunts me,
Her taunts are all I see,
Nyx has sent her servants forth,
They seek me out in force.
The nightmares follow me around,
They are with me day and night,
I hear your voice's laughing sound,
And I see your scorned delight.
I see the dreams within my dreams,
Nightmares among my terrors,
What hope remains to yet redeem,
From my world of pain and errors?

Beyond the twilight and the dusk,

When the moon is silver lust,

What images are here to trust,

In these traumas which I am thrust

But the dream within my nightmare,

The face that calls my soul,

The smiling face and loving stare,

That seeks to make me whole?

I try to catch your willing eyes

Upon the face my sleep supplies,

But you turn so coldly away from me,

Ignore my desperate plea.

Index

About the Author

Ian McGrath is a long-time poet and author of *Veiled Nightmares & Ethereal Dreams*, which is a unique exploration of how the spiritual and non-spiritual collide in the semi-conscious and our dreams, and how our dreams can affect us in daily life. It is his first published anthology, but hopefully not his last; Ian has over a thousand 'finished' poems and this is hopefully but a taste of what he can do. He hopes to follow this sombre look at some of the darker range of emotions with a more mystical and love themed anthology titled *Crystal Hearts & Glass Souls*. With over a decade writing and performing poetry in and around Widnes and Liverpool, Ian is a hidden gem who has only recently decided to share his work with the world. Ian is also an experienced fire and circus performer, specialising in staff and double contact staff. A drummer in high school who has switched to guitar, Ian favours a melodic style of rhyming poetry.

Beaten Track Publishing

For more titles from Beaten Track Publishing,
please visit our website:

https://www.beatentrackpublishing.com

Thanks for reading!